Why, Charlie Brown, Why?

A Story About What Happens
When a Friend is Very Ill

created by
Charles M. Schulz

Introduction by Gary Lineker

RAVETTE PUBLISHING

This edition published by Ravette Publishing 2005

Printed and bound in Belgium
for Ravette Publishing Limited
Unit 3, Tristar Centre,
Star Road, Partridge Green,
West Sussex RH13 8RA

ISBN: 1 84161 231 6

Every 48 hours, 10 children in the UK are diagnosed with cancer or leukaemia. The services that CLIC Sargent (the UK's leading children's cancer charity) provide, help children and young people to understand what they are going through. They also support the whole family every step of the way.

When children get cancer or leukaemia, they often feel very different from their friends. I have met many children, young people and their families who often feel alone and bewildered as they go through their treatment.

This book is designed to explain to young people what happens when someone gets cancer. You will read here how Charlie Brown, Linus and the rest of the Peanuts gang begin to understand a little about cancer and a lot about life.

I know that 'Why, Charlie Brown, Why?' is a great way for young people to understand more about cancer.

Gary Lineker

*I*t was a beautiful cool, clear autumn morning, just chilly enough so that the children waiting for the school bus were wearing their jackets. Charlie Brown's sister, Sally, was complaining, as usual.

"Some day there will be a monument right here, and you know what it will say? It will say, 'Here is where Sally Brown wasted the best years of her life, waiting for the school bus.'"

Linus was talking with Janice, a little girl with beautiful blonde hair who had moved into the neighbourhood several months ago. She sat behind Linus in class.

"Did you enjoy the swings yesterday, Janice?"

"I sure did," said Janice. "I love the swings, and you are the best swing pusher in school."

"Well," said Linus, "it's fun pushing you because you go higher than anybody else."

Charlie Brown's dog, Snoopy, was hanging around with them, of course, and when the school bus finally pulled up to the kerb, he was the first one to jump in.

Unfortunately, the driver booted him out immediately.

"Sorry," explained Charlie Brown. "You can't go with us. Dogs aren't allowed on the school bus."

"Woof," said Snoopy.

Snoopy was not about to get left behind, though. He hurried around to the rear of the bus and jumped up onto the back bumper, where he happily played his harmonica.

As Janice climbed the steps into the bus, she bumped her elbow on the railing. "Ow," she groaned. "Great! Now I'll have another bruise."

She held her arm out to show Linus. "Look, I bumped myself last week and the bruise is still there. Look at all the bruises on my legs."

"You do have a lot of bruises."

"I know," said Janice. "I feel so clumsy."

When the children got off the bus and walked onto the school grounds, Linus asked Janice if she would like to be pushed on a swing before they went in.

"I don't think so, Linus," she said. "I'm not sure I feel well today, but thank you anyway."

"Is it your stomach?" asked Linus. "Maybe it's just nerves. I always get a stomach-ache when I know we're going to have a test."

Janice shrugged. "Maybe."

Later, even after they were seated at their desks, Janice still did not seem herself. Linus asked, "Are you all right?"

"I don't know," replied Janice. "I've just been feeling so tired lately. Feel my head, will you, Linus? Is it warm? I think I may have a fever."

He reached back and felt her forehead with the palm of his hand. "Yes," he said. "It is a little warm. If you don't feel well, maybe you should go see the nurse."

"I suppose I should," she said. So just before class started, Janice got up from her desk and walked slowly across the room, out the door, and down the hall to the nurse's office. There, her temperature was taken by the nurse and found to be 39°C. Janice agreed that she should call her mother to come and pick her up to take her home. In the meantime, her form teacher asked Linus what he had been talking about with Janice.

"Well, Miss," he said. "She wasn't feeling well, so I told her she should go see the nurse...No, Miss, I'm not a doctor."

Several days went by, the weather grew a little colder, and the children found themselves waiting for the school bus without Janice.

"I don't know, Charlie Brown," said Linus. "I haven't heard a word from her since the day she went to see the school nurse."

As usual, Sally was complaining. "Why does everyone worry so much about Janice? I'm the one who's going to have a bad day."

"Why is that?" asked Charlie Brown.

"Because I left my lunch sitting on the kerb."

This was, of course, just the sort of break Snoopy waited for. As a dog, he felt that anything left behind belonged to him and in no time at all, he was enjoying a wonderful early morning snack.

27

That morning, Linus's teacher was finally able to explain to everyone why Janice had not returned to class. Janice was in the hospital. She would not be returning to school for a while. After school in the afternoon, Charlie Brown and Linus, being very thoughtful, decided to visit their friend. They were a little surprised to see Snoopy walking down one of the hospital corridors dressed as the world famous surgeon. Of course, they had long ago become used to his strange actions. They were slightly puzzled, however, when they saw him running furiously up and down several flights of stairs.

"Why is the world famous surgeon running up and down the stairs like that, Charlie Brown?"

"I imagine it's because he can't reach the lift buttons."

The two boys found Janice's room. She was delighted to see them. "Our teacher told us you were in the hospital," said Linus. "Your fever must have been awful."

Janice held up her arm. A needle was attached to it. "It wasn't just a fever," she said. "I have cancer."

"Cancer?" exclaimed Linus. "I don't understand. How do they know that?"

"Well," said Janice, "they've done lots of tests on me. They found out that I have leukaemia. That's why I had all those bruises. My blood has cancer in it."

"You're not going to die, are you?" asked Charlie Brown.

"Good grief!" said Linus. "What kind of a question is that?"

"That's all right," said Janice. "I asked the doctors the same question. They took several blood tests and I even had a bone marrow test. Leukaemia cells live deep inside my bones where blood is made. They stuck a needle right here into the bone to take some marrow out."

"Oh, no!" said Linus. "That must've hurt a lot!"

"Well, yes," said Janice. "I suppose it did, but first they numb your skin, and anyway, it didn't last long. Now they have me hooked up to this drip. It's a way of giving me chemotherapy. This medicine will probably help me, but they tell me it could also make my hair fall out. Please don't worry. I know I'm going to get better because I want to get back to school and swing on those swings."

"You get better, Janice," said Linus, "and I'll push you on those swings forever."

It was early evening as the boys walked slowly home. A lot had happened to them in their short lives, but this was the first time they had ever faced anything serious. Linus, especially, felt an ache within himself unlike anything he had ever known. He realized how much Janice meant to him as a friend, and the more he thought about it, the less he felt he could understand what was happening.

As they paused before leaving each other, Linus turned and said, "Why, Charlie Brown, why?"

This time, Charlie Brown had no answer, and Linus walked slowly away.

When Linus got home, his sister, Lucy, was sitting in front of the TV set.

"Charlie Brown and I were visiting Janice in the hospital," he said. "She has leukaemia."

"While you're up," said Lucy, "why don't you get me a glass of milk?"

Linus turned quickly, went to the kitchen, poured the milk for Lucy, and brought it to her. "I remember that day," he said, "when she wasn't feeling well. I remember touching her forehead and feeling how warm she was."

"You touched her forehead?" shouted Lucy. "And now you're handing me a glass of milk? You could catch leukaemia from her and give it to me!"

"Cancer is not contagious," said Linus. "You can't catch it from somebody like a cold or flu."

"She probably got it," said Lucy, "because she's a bit weird."

"Janice did not get cancer because of something she did wrong. It just happened."

"Well, anyway," said Lucy, handing the glass to Linus, "take the milk back."

"No, thank you," said Linus. "I don't want to catch your crabbiness!"

Autumn turned quickly into winter that year, and soon the streets were covered with snow. The children were waiting for the school bus. It turned out to be a very special morning, for Janice suddenly appeared, wearing a new pink cap.

"You're back!" cried Linus, barely containing his glee. "You've been away from school for a long time. Is everything okay? Are you better now?"

"Well, I think I'm getting better," replied Janice. "My doctor says I'm doing great."

When the bus arrived, they boarded together.

"They've put the swings away for the winter," said Linus. "I'm sorry. I was looking forward to giving you a good push on the swings."

"That's all right," said Janice. "There'll be another time for that."

When they got to school, an obnoxious-looking boy ran up and shouted, "Hey, nice hat! Pretty cool! Does it fly? I think it needs a propeller," and he reached up and knocked the pink cap from Janice's head. Janice tried to cover her head with her hands, but it was too late. Everybody on the playground, including Linus, saw that her hair was gone.

"Hey, look at this!" the obnoxious boy shouted. "A baldie!"

Tears filled Janice's eyes. When Linus saw this, all of the emotion that had been building up inside him came pouring out, and he shouted furiously at the obnoxious boy, "What's the matter with you? Huh? What's the matter?"

"What's the matter with me?" shouted the boy. "What's the matter with her? She's bald! She's got no hair!"

Linus grabbed the front of the bully's shirt and shook him furiously. "Janice has leukaemia, cement head! That's cancer. Have you ever heard of cancer? She's been in the hospital. She's had chemotherapy to help her get better and it made her hair fall out. Does that make you happy? Would you like to go through what she's gone through? Think about it, or don't you ever think about anything?"

Linus and Janice turned to walk away. As they did, the boy picked up the cap and said very sheepishly, "I'm sorry." Then he suddenly brightened. "Hey, it really is a nice cap," he said.

At school, some of the other students in her class were talking about the extra attention that Janice was now getting.

"See," one whispered to another. "The teacher is always being extra nice to Janice. How does she get away with it?"

All day Linus defended her, of course. "You don't know what you're talking about. If she gets special treatment, it's because she's been sick."

Early that evening, Charlie Brown was sitting in his favourite chair reading when Snoopy opened the door and walked into the room with a long extension cord. He unplugged the lamp next to Charlie Brown and plugged in his own extension cord. Immediately, all of the Christmas tree lights that he had strung around his doghouse lit up, and he now had the most beautifully decorated home in the neighbourhood.

At the same time, Linus was taking the Christmas present he had bought for Janice over to her house. When he knocked on the door, a little girl answered.

"Hi," said Linus. "Is Janice at home? I'm Linus. I sit in front of her at school."

"I'm Janice's little sister. She's not at home. She had to go back for more treatment, but I think she'll come home again tomorrow."

Another girl joined them at the door and said, "Hi. What's going on? I'm Janice's older sister."

"This is Linus," said the little girl. "He's brought Janice a present."

"Another present?" said the older sister. "Everyone brings Janice something. She gets more presents than the two of us together, and we have to be so careful around her. We can't even get chicken pox. If we did, she would catch it from us and it would be really bad for her. Actually, she's becoming a real nuisance."

"You don't really mean that, do you?" said Linus. "She's your sister."

"Well, I don't know. I suppose not. It's just that we've been feeling a little left out lately since Janice got leukaemia."

The two sisters took Linus's present inside and placed it with all of the others under the tree. "She gets a lot of presents, though."

"Well," said Linus, "maybe that's a way for people to show they hope she gets better."

After the holidays, Janice's desk remained empty. The weeks went by, and the weather grew warmer. Finally, one early spring morning, Janice returned to the bus stop.

"Janice, you're back!" said Linus. "How do you feel?"

"Much better, thank you. I can't believe I've been inside so long."

Charlie Brown said, "We're all glad you're back. It was sad seeing your empty desk when you were away having treatment."

"I missed being in school," said Janice.

A few weeks later at the school playground, Linus led Janice to the swings that had finally been put up again after the long winter. "See," he said. "They're up! The swings are up again!"

"I have a surprise for you, Linus," said Janice, as she climbed up onto the swing. "But, first, push me. Push me, Linus!"

Carefully, he pulled her back and gave her a big push.

"Higher!" shouted Janice. "Push me higher!"

He pushed her harder, and she began to swing up and up, and Linus shouted, "What's the surprise?"

As the swing rose high into the morning sunlight, Janice tilted her head back and let the wind catch under the peak of her pink cap. Suddenly, it flew off, and her beautiful blonde hair swirled free behind her.

Linus shouted out, then yelled a cheer and Janice laughed, and the cap she'd worn all winter long, the cap she wouldn't need to wear any longer, fell quietly to the ground. Janice was back!

A Little Help with Medical Terms

Acute: occurring suddenly or over a short period of time.

Alopecia: hair loss.

Anaemic: low number of red blood cells.

Benign Tumour: a non-cancerous growth that does not spread to other parts of the body.

Biopsy: a small sample of the body tissue is removed and examined under a microscope.

Bone Marrow: spongy material found in the centre of bones, produces blood cells.

Cancer: a general term for about 100 diseases characterised by uncontrolled, abnormal growth of cells.

Carcinogen: a chemical or other agent that causes cancer.

Chemotherapy: the use of drugs to destroy cancer cells.

Chronic: a term that is used to describe a disease of long duration or one that is progressing slowly.

Cytotoxic Drugs: anti-cancer drugs.

Diagnosis: identify actual type of disease from symptoms, tests and investigations of patient.

Haemoglobin: (Hb) part of the red blood cell; contains iron and helps to carry oxygen around the body.

Immune System: the body's system of defences against disease, composed of certain white blood cells and antibodies. Antibodies are protein substances that react against bacteria and other harmful material.

Intravenous: to give drugs or fluids directly into a vein.

Leukaemia: a cancer of the blood cells.

Lymphoma: a cancer of the lymphatic system (which contains the lymph nodes/glands).

Malignant: cancerous. The abnormal/cancer cells are able to spread to other parts of the body if not treated.

Metastases: the spread of cancer cells from the original site (primary) to other parts of the body (secondaries).

Neutrophil: a type of white blood cell.

Neutropenic: a low number of neutrophils/white blood cells.

Oncology: the study of cancer.

Petechiae: small pin-prick bruises, from tiny blood vessels just beneath the skin.

Platelets: tiny cells which help to clot the blood to prevent bleeding and bruising.

Prognosis: the prediction of the outcome of the disease.

Protocol: plan of treatment.

Radiotherapy: the use of radiation treatment or high energy rays which destroy the cancer cells, while doing as little harm as possible to normal cells.

Red Blood Cells: they carry oxygen around the body and also contain iron.

Relapse: when the disease comes back after a period of time when symptoms had disappeared or decreased.

Remission: a healthy state when all the abnormal cancer cells can no longer be detected.

Surgery: to have an operation.

Transfusion: fluids or blood products given as an infusion into the vein using a drip.

Thrombocytopenic: a low number of platelets in the blood.

Tumour: a growth of abnormal tissue which grows at a faster rate than normal tissue and serves no function there.

White Blood Cells: main fighting cells of the blood which help to fight off infections.

X-rays: high-energy radiation used in high doses to treat cancer or in low doses to diagnose the disease.

Created with the help of CLIC Sargent